Maureen,

"Speak up for those who cannot speak for themselves; ensure justice for those being crushed. Yes, speak up for the poor and helpless and see that they get justice." Proverbs 31:8-9 NLT

Wanda

Trilogy Christian Publishers
A Wholly Owned Subsidiary of Trinity Broadcasting Network
2442 Michelle Drive
Tustin, CA 92780
Copyright © 2023 by Wanda Moore Anker

Scripture quotations marked KJV are taken from The Holy Bible, King James Version. Cambridge Edition: 1769.

Scripture quotations marked niv are taken from the Holy Bible, New International Version®, NIV®. Copyright © 1973, 1978, 1984, 2011 by Biblica, Inc. TM Used by permission of Zondervan. All rights reserved worldwide. www.zondervan.com. The "NIV" and "New International Version" are trademarks registered in the United States Patent and Trademark Office by Biblica, Inc.TM
Scripture quotations marked nkjv are taken from the New King James Version®. Copyright © 1982 by Thomas Nelson. Used by permission. All rights reserved.
Scripture quotations marked nlt are taken from the Holy Bible, New Living Translation, copyright © 1996, 2004, 2015 by Tyndale House Foundation. Used by permission of Tyndale House Publishers, Inc., Carol Stream, Illinois 60188. All rights reserved.
All rights reserved, including the right to reproduce this book or portions thereof in any form whatsoever.
For information, address Trilogy Christian Publishing
Rights Department, 2442 Michelle Drive, Tustin, CA 92780.

Trilogy Christian Publishing/TBN and colophon are trademarks of Trinity Broadcasting Network.
For information about special discounts for bulk purchases, please contact Trilogy Christian Publishing.
Manufactured in the United States of America
Trilogy Disclaimer: The views and content expressed in this book are those of the author and may not necessarily reflect the views and doctrine of Trilogy Christian Publishing or the Trinity Broadcasting Network.
10 9 8 7 6 5 4 3 2 1
Library of Congress Cataloging-in-Publication Data is available.
ISBN 979-8-89041-326-0
ISBN (ebook) 979-8-89041-327-7

BROKEN

A Journey Through Long-Term Care

Wanda Moore Anker

Introduction

WRITING THIS BOOK FLOODS MY SOUL WITH heartache, brokenness, and sadness, just as it painfully felt with each encounter during the past five years. My situation was not in my control but felt out of control. Many times, over and over and over, I cried constantly. I prayed constantly. The same prayer: "Lord, I don't even know where to begin."

I share my personal story with a burden assigned to me by the Holy Spirit to write a convenient- sized devotional that can be easily carried and is filled with words of encouragement, scriptures of support, and examples of prayers that has been designed to walk with you through your heartache, brokenness, and sadness. I trust that if you are in a situation of responsibility and making decisions for a loved one in or needing long-term care that my story will leap off the written page and into your heart bringing peace and healing and maybe… someday… even joy.

Here is my story. The following pages are devotions for you to read with scriptures for you to meditate and memorize, followed by a prayer to give you peace through your journey.

Every Saturday I would get off work and drive a 60-mile round trip to have lunch and visit my mother, Geraldine, who was 79 years old at the time, and my brother, William, who was 62 years old. It was January of 2018 that everything in each of our lives changed in an instant. William, who was our mom's 24/7 caregiver, suffered a severe brain bleed and a stroke in the central area of his brain at their home and was being life flighted to a hospital in Pittsburgh, sixty miles, one way, before I could reach their home. I immediately had to fill in. No warning. No planning. No written schedule of meds and times to administer them. Nothing!

Accelerating the story, William was in the ICU for weeks as they tried to stabilize his blood pressure to prevent another stroke. The days before this were active. He had just purchased a new car and had been taking full responsibility for Mom's care for the last 14 years since our father passed away. He was now left totally paralyzed on the right side of his body, cognitively slow in speech and movement, with swallowing issues, and was soon moved to a rehabilitation facility even further from my home. My life began the intense stress of trying to manage my brother's situation, decisions and life disappointments added to the facility meetings with the rehab team, billing departments, attorneys and oh, I forgot to mention that he did not have health insurance.

My personal stress level at this time was spiraling into what felt like a nervous breakdown at 3 a.m., sleeping in a recliner next to my mom in her living room. You see, she wasn't well either, with anxiety or depression issues that she fought her whole life. She had been hospitalized many times and could not be left alone. My older brother and I were the only immediate family members remaining.

Allow me to share at this time that my husband and I are entrepreneurs in three different businesses, and I could not afford to deal with the hand that I was just dealt. The "divine interruption," as some would call it, did not adequately describe my current situation.

Two weeks since the stroke and I had no choice but to place my mom into a long-term care facility. I was now dealing with two family members in different care facilities at the same time and sixty miles one way from each other.

Fast forwarding for the sake of this introduction and more details, as you read the book, I will share how Jesus provided, how Jesus picked me up and used my favorite mentor in the Bible, Nehemiah, to impress upon my life the "burden" of his calling placed on him by the Lord. His position of constant prayer and most importantly, for me anyway, was building a "community" of support of family, friends, colleagues, medical staff, attorneys, social workers, business managers and facility directors from the first weeks of true feelings that I did not know where to even begin this journey. I was filled with feelings of brokenness and suffering. I constantly repeated these words... "Really, Lord! I can't do this!!!"

I need to share that all of this happened one year before the COVID-19 pandemic which turned our world inside out and isolated me from my mom and brother. More brokenness!! My heart was ripped out each day with no visits, no church programs on Sunday, no communion or singing that my mom looked forward to each week. Grooming appointments ended. Everything ended abruptly!

My mom passed away during the continued pandemic on September 10, 2020, and my brother on March 21, 2022.

It is with great passion that I write this book from a platform that did not come with an instruction manual. I pray that it will be an encouragement to your heart and life, that the stories will find you where you are in the journey of caregiving and brokenness. I trust that you will also feel the presence of Jesus carrying you and even delivering you from one of the hardest "interruptions" one could encounter in life's journey.

He is our Shepherd and will lead you to places of peace and help when walking through the valleys. One of my favorite scriptures that I have stood on is found in Ecclesiastes 7:8 KJV, "Better is the end of a thing than the beginning." I'm sure that it will become one of your favorites too!!

#

Contents

1. The Staff!! 11
2. Administration Process 13
3. I Don't Even Know Where to Start! 15
4. ANGELS UNAWARE! 17
5. Nervous Breakdown!! 19
6. Support: Build a Community 21
7. Dementia and Other Medical Issues 23
8. Not the Same Person: Covid Arrives 25
9. Visitation Dates 27
10. "Death is a Process" 29
11. Pick Your Battles 33
12. Brokenness and Suffering 35
13. GUILT 37
14. Resources That Help 39
15. New Titles, Decisions and End of Life 41
16. Stress – Taking Care of Yourself 43
17. A "New Normal" 45
18. Heaven's Roll Call 47
19. It's the Small Things 49
20. Jesus Loves the Little Children and So Do the Elderly . . 51
21. Memories 53
22. A New Set of Wheels 55
23. 'Tis the Season – Room and Holiday Decorations 57

24.	Gift of Giving: Birthdays, Special Occasions, Etc.	59
25.	Isolation and Deterioration (Covid 19)	61
26.	Transition – It's a Process	63
27.	How to Make a No Sew Tied Blanket	65
28.	What Do Faith, Church, Ministries, and Pets Have in Common?	69
29.	It's a Beautiful Day. Rediscover Life	71
30.	Life is Like a Box of Chocolates	73
31.	Final Chapter – William's Death	75

#

Chapter One: The Staff!!

Colossians 3:23-24 NKJV, "And whatever you do, do it heartily, as to the Lord and not to men, knowing that from the Lord you will receive the reward of the inheritance, for you serve the Lord Christ."

THIS DEVOTION SPEAKS OF THE STAFF/EXTENDED family of long-term care facilities. The staff knows our loved one like you do. My mom loved to be dressed every day, complete with earrings and shoes. If it was a holiday or season change, that would include celebrating with accessories too! The staff made sure that this was a priority for her. Mom had a favorite CD of my uncle singing with his guitar. She didn't comprehend how to turn the player off and save batteries.

My mother loved her Pastor Rufus Peer and the visits of church friends with snacks or who sang hymns with her. During the "lockdown" of COVID 19, outside visits were not allowed and all outside entertainment and inside group entertainment came to a halt which meant no weekly church service. She read her Bible every day and her faith in God was important to her. I asked that they make sure that the TV channel was set on gospel music or a Christian radio station was on for her.

I realized that I was asking for tasks above and beyond their daily assignments. I appreciate that the staff cared and were compassionate enough to take my place when I couldn't be there.

Thank them often! Donate cupcakes at holiday or birthday times. Donate money to the activities department. Develop relationships with them. They have family and life outside of work too.

Prayer: Heavenly Father, thank You for the staff that is taking care of my mom. Thank You for the heart of compassion, care, and love to go above and beyond their daily tasks and work "as unto You." In Jesus' name, amen.

#

Chapter Two: Administration Process

Psalm 120:1 NKJV, "In my distress I cried to the Lord, and he heard me."

I DROVE DOWN THE ROAD WITH TEARS FLOWING and not even cognizant of WHERE to begin this process of long-term care for one person, let alone two! My continual conversation with God began with "*Lord, I don't know WHERE to start.*"

The "Admin Process" is just that. Meetings…in tears most of the time… paperwork…attorneys…added to daily responsibilities of keeping up with paying bills, bank account authorization, prescription refills. Your own life STOPS so that you can pick up where they left off!

Unfortunately, I failed to mention that I was the only family member left of my immediate family and my brother was in the ICU, 60 miles away from a massive stroke. Not that it matters, but my age at the time was 58 years old, still employed and an entrepreneur.

My advice is to surround yourself with healthcare people, an elder attorney, people of faith/clergy, and even the director of your family funeral establishment. You need to develop a relationship with these professionals within their specialized fields of assistance to you.

You can do this! Remember the story of the footprints in the sand? Even when you don't feel the Lord, He is carrying you and when you look back, you will see only one set of footprints behind you. He has promised to never leave you nor forsake you. You can stand on that promise!

Lastly, I encourage you to take a participative position with the long-term care facility. Attend the scheduled care meetings. Ask questions (remember, they are the professionals and see these situations every day). Take notes. Keep a journal to track important dates of appointments, legal papers filed, etc.

Prayer: Lord, under Your wings will I hide until these calamities pass by. Heal my heart from the constant feeling of brokenness and lead me in this process of administration. I ask that You give me favor with each decision that I must make.

#

Chapter Three: I Don't Even Know Where to Start!

Psalm 121:1-2 NKJV, "I will lift up my eyes to the hills. From whence comes my help? My help comes from the Lord, who made heaven and earth."

LIFE DOESN'T COME WITH A ROAD MAP! I'LL NEVER forget the feeling I had when driving in my car, heading towards town, and saying out loud to God ... *"I don't even know where to start."* My mom was admitted to the hospital and needed to go to a facility that would meet her needs and my brother would soon move into rehab center after ICU and physical therapy. He was our mother's twenty-four-hour caregiver for 14 years prior to his stroke. Who do you call to help with this emergency?! What agencies are there to assist you? Questions always finish with "How much will it cost?"

I felt hopeless, my heart broken in a zillion pieces to see Mom deal with the challenge of my brother in the ICU, was he going to make it? He was 60 miles from Mom, and we were without a map for what was ahead of us!

Where did I start? How can I help you today? For me, first was PRAYER and my family pastor. Second was the social worker at the hospital who was able to start with a list of facilities and agencies for our support. A few suggestions for you are: your local Agency on Aging, your church fellowship; local home health care agencies and don't forget opportunities from your friends on social media.

Prayer: Oh, Holy Jesus, the cavity of my chest seems like a huge hole! My heart is broken in a million pieces and my lungs feel empty; it's hard to breathe. I cry unto You to help me. Lead me to the place that You have for my mom. Give me favor with them and mostly, please, Lord, give me peace that is beyond my own understanding.

Chapter Four: ANGELS UNAWARE!

> Psalm 91:11 NKJV, "For he shall give his angels charge over you, to keep you in all your ways."

My life came to a sudden halt with a broken heart, and suffering was constant! My daily prayers kept pleading with God with requests to help me, to provide someone to help me to sit with my mom while I'm in the ICU with my brother who is 60 miles away (one way). My requests included the money to pay someone. I cried CONSTANTLY!! I felt helpless, stressed, and had to get a grip.

My daughter called and texted me with the name of someone who attends her church. This lady was in the health care industry, a nurse from NY who was in PA helping her sister and her mom while she was on FMLA (family medical leave). Oh, how Jesus answered that prayer! An angel, unaware. Not only did she sit with Mom – she loved it. She read the Bible to my mom and prayed with her. You see, my mom was going through her own battles with my brother gone since he oversaw her care, medications, meals, and everyday needs. They were never apart.

To you who are reading this, my encouragement to you is to let your requests be made known and trust Jesus to answer. Look around for those angels we are unaware of, angels who have been put in charge of us. The Lord already knows your needs before you ask.

Prayer: I thank You, Heavenly Father, that You hear my prayers and answer them, that you provide for our every need, that You comfort us and whisper Your words of "Peace, be still."

Chapter Five: Nervous Breakdown!!

Psalm 118:5 KJV, "I called to the Lord out of my distress, and he answered me."

It was around 3:00 a.m; the season was winter, in the month of February. I had to stay with mom 24/7, away from my own working responsibilities, my own house, cooking, and cleaning. Just trying to figure out what my mom's medications were and what needed to be filled, etc. was a huge challenge. Not able to leave her alone, the nighttime became my only personal time of prayer, tears, and dealing with the mental stress of the day.

I began to feel like ants were crawling all over me. The first night I wrote it off as catching the flu. I was shaking and lacking energy. Second night.... Repeat!! Not having flu symptoms during the day, I realized that I may be having a nervous breakdown myself! This can't be!!!

Hiding my bright phone screen under my blanket, I began to text with a cousin of mine about what was happening. We went to prayer, standing on the promises of the Word of God. The tingly,

.t-crawling feeling began to leave. I needed to get myself to a place of planning instead of worry. The tears still didn't stop. The brokenness I felt in my heart… still there. Constant! Daily! Hourly! Moment by moment.

If this is your present position while reading this book or you chose this chapter for a specific reason, my prayers are with you. I pray that you will see that God is on your side. Know that He will provide whatever you need, and you can stand on His promises. He will see you through.

Dear Lord, I am so grateful that You promised that You would never leave me nor forsake me. At this very present time, I need Your presence. I need Your touch of healing. Deliver me from this near-overcoming illness and anxiety attack from the enemy. Thank You for Your unconditional love.

Chapter Six: Support: Build Community

Nehemiah 1:11 NKJV, "O Lord, I pray, please let your ear be attentive to the prayer of your servant, and to the prayer of our servants who desire to fear your name; and let your servant prosper this day, I pray, and grant him mercy."

I REACHED OUT TO FOUR OF MY FRIENDS. My request was for each of them to come one Sunday within the next four Sundays to anoint and pray for me through this awful sickness of anxiety and stress. I was sick for months. Stomach nausea took over and for three months all I ate was crackers, applesauce, and yogurt, with ginger ale to drink while trying to settle the overwhelming nausea. I lost thirty-two pounds.

One of my favorites in the Bible is Nehemiah. It was brought to my attention that during his assignment to rebuild the walls of Jerusalem, he also felt overwhelmed and that he couldn't take on this huge task by himself. So, he first prayed to the Lord and then he began to build a community of people to do this with him.

Here is a list of things that I did, and I encourage you to build your community to support you as well. To pray with you, celebrate with you, and give you time away and still meet your loved one's needs.

Involve your church pastors and leaders. Our pastor was 95 years old and would drive with me to pray and give communion to my brother and my mother.

Ask family and friends to volunteer their time or ministry. One friend loved art and would paint with my mom on a weekly scheduled visit. Another one sang hymns with my mom during her visits.

Social media has a lot to offer and it's free! I would post a birthday announcement with addresses, then read to her when visiting.

Invite your friends and family to bring their animals to visit. There are policies on this to check out first, but the residents LOVE their animals and love to tell you about them!

Dance costumes were always enjoyed by the residents. My granddaughter would wear her tutu and tights to visit my mom and the joy in Mom's smile and eyes was indescribable.

Dear Jesus, thank You for happy days. Thank You for sunny days. Thank You for friends and family with the heart to volunteer, show love, and to serve. I ask You to bless the seeds of love and kindness that each visitor sows into the lives of our loved ones. Thank You for the much-needed breaks in our stressful schedules while providing care for our loved ones.

Chapter Seven: Dementia and Other Medical Issues

Isaiah 26:3 NLT, "You will keep him in perfect peace, whose minds are steadfast, because they trust in you."

I BEGAN TO SEE MEDICAL CHANGES IN MY MOM. The first was dementia, a slow disease that results in losing a relationship with your loved one. We all feel forgetfulness occasionally as we age. It can be funny at times and embarrassing when you can't remember the name of someone that you know who is right in front of you. Dementia is sad. It is slow. It is irreversible. It highlights your feelings of brokenness. One of the strongest challenges that I had at this time was the answer to the question, do I correct my mom when she calls another female resident her sister's name, Brenda, when her name is Catherine, and she is not her sister? Or to call out my brother when he would tell me that his friend called him, and I would check his phone and see that there weren't any calls. These times, which were many, were very sad. To answer the question of correcting them, no, there isn't much enjoyment in their lives. I would see their sadness when I tried to correct them. It's not worth it.

Medical conditions continued with many UTI's, swallowing difficulties, chronic kidney failure from dehydration, the list grows longer. The worry was constant. I spent hours on the internet reading, taking notes, and writing questions for the scheduled care meetings for both.

It can be physically draining and cause unbearable exhaustion at times. I trust that these experiences of mine will make your journey easier. Remember that this a season in your life. It isn't forever, although it truly feels like there is no end when each day has its own battle. I believe that the Lord gives us the strength that we need for each day.

Heavenly Father, sometimes my prayers seem to be on a repeat button. I am weary today and don't feel that I have the strength to do this. Help me to understand this condition of dementia and provide for me all that I need to make it through this day.

Chapter Eight: Not the Same Person: Covid Arrives

Psalms 55:1-2 NLT, "Listen to my prayer, O God. Do not ignore my cry for help! Please listen and answer me for I am overwhelmed by my troubles."

I HAVE WATCHED MOM DECLINE FIRST MENTALLY, physically with difficulty swallowing, and then not eating, weight loss, always sleeping and having no desire to get out of bed. These symptoms appeared in the last six months since COVID arrived! I remember an outside doctor appointment for a broken femur. This was the first time for Mom to experience the requirement of having a mask on properly. With sadness in her voice and eyes, she said, "Things aren't the same anymore." She briefly spoke of experiences of the Great Depression in her young days when she had no control to make things better.

These days were her first times of experiencing abundant sadness!! Deep depression followed. No socialization, group activities, or bingo. She kept her deep Christian faith with Bible preaching and singing with volunteers who came to share hymns and play the piano for the residents all gathered in a circle, each in their own wheelchair.

Grooming was important to my mom. I scheduled regular hair appointments, and she would enjoy a perm and haircut every six weeks or so. She loved having her nails painted and to be up and dressed every day. I remember one Facetime call that brought me to tears. It was the first Facetime call since COVID. I watched her choke back the tears in sadness as she could see herself in the camera, her hair long and without curls, not dressed in matching clothing. There were feelings of constant brokenheartedness. Along with the others, she did not understand or comprehend the new rules or not being able to visit with us. She was changed forever from that moment on.

If long-term care is your cross to carry currently, my prayers are with you. I encourage you to step out of feelings of brokenness and continue to make a difference in their lives even when in the circumstances of disappointment. When you can't be there, send flowers, cards, food baskets, and pictures.

Holy Father. I come to You today in prayer for those who are amid the challenges of long-term care, those that are broken and discouraged, those who are tired and feel hopeless. Remind them of Your eternal promises to one day be with You in Heaven, delivered from the sins and calamities of this earth. I ask that You give them joy, hope, physical and mental strength every day, in Jesus' name.

Chapter Nine: Visitation Dates

> Matthew 25:40 NIV, "Truly I tell you, whatever you did for one of the least of these brothers and sisters of mine, you did for me."

Visitation dates had to be scheduled on my calendar since I still worked and had other commitments. Not to forget that my brother was in long-term care at the same time, so double the need to be at two different places each week.

I encourage you with a few ideas that I did to make the visits brighter. I tried to include friends and family to take a turn and help to spread a little sunshine in my mom's and brother's routine as well as to give me a break.

Picnics: my cousin would come in and have a picnic with my mom in her room. I purchased a small three basket organizer that fit in her closet. In my brother's room, I used an empty drawer. Each was the perfect size to hold several kinds of snacks, chocolates, and beverages.

Arts and crafts: my mom liked to paint with a small paint brush. She made bookmarkers out of felt. I added a hanging clothesline with sparkly pins to display her artwork.

Pastor visits: my mom's pastor, already in his 90's at the time, loved to see her. At her funeral he shared that when he was walking down the hall toward her room, he could hear these welcoming words… "Here comes my pastor!"

Family and children: I cannot put into words how much those away from family and in long- term situations desire to see their families, and particularly grandchildren. My youngest granddaughter would climb up in bed with my mom and play with her decorative stuffed pillows. Another granddaughter would paint my mom's nails.

Birthdays and celebrations: it was fun to purchase several dozen cupcakes to share with other residents and staff to celebrate their big day. A table centerpiece adds a beautiful touch that you can leave with them. (I have a birthday note to share with you. In the interim of the last three years of Mom's life and my brother's stroke, she only saw him one time. It was on her birthday that we transported her by wheelchair to the rehabilitation facility that he was in to celebrate with lunch and cake).

Dear Jesus, thank You for always being with us. I ask that You bless each one reading this devotional today. Provide for the needs of the family and friends so that they can create joyful times and beautiful memories in one of the most heart-breaking experiences in their lives.

Chapter Ten: "Death is a Process"

Psalm 23:4 NIV, "Even though I walk through the darkest valley, I will fear no evil, for you are with me; your rod and your staff, they comfort me."

I HAVE TWO DAUGHTERS AND BOTH WORK IN SOME capacity in the medical field. My younger, a respiratory therapy specialist, works in the hospitals. Many times, it is nice to have a family member with a background in health care. However, I experienced that they also have a "bedside manner" when it comes to conversations of health issues, etc. The conversation seems to be more "factual" than "friendly" at times. I was discussing a few ailments that I was experiencing and to my surprise, my younger daughter bluntly said, "Mom, death is a process, and your body is slowly dying now that you have passed 50 years of age. It is going the other way now."

Well, okay! I watched this "process" with both my mom and brother. First was the cognitive decline, the memories of things not there any longer. Then there was the physical decline of weakness and aging. The UTI's started multiple rounds of infection and hospitalization. Falls and broken bones of the femur, wrist, and my brother broke off four of his front teeth when trying to transition himself with assistance.

Death approached, and wasn't expected in either of them at the last time of their hospitalizations. Sepsis had set in following infections. High doses of antibiotics and pain meds were given hoping to control the situation. Organs began to fail, and hours became a time of waiting for a miracle of healing.

In one of my conversations with my mom, she told me that when she was dying, "Don't pray me back because I'm going to be with Jesus in heaven and have no more pain." She assured me that she loved me but that she didn't want to stay here. When she was dying, I played hymns on my phone to help both of us. Her breathing was rushed and her eyes moved as if she was looking for someone or something. Her breathing slowed to a peaceful rate. It was at that very moment that she walked into heaven with her last breath.

My brother ended up in hospice care in the hospital. Eyes closed, steady breathing, and the only peace I could feel was thinking that he was never going to be in pain, hospitalized or live in long-term care again. He would be free from the last four years.

There is much more to this "process" including a living will, pre-funeral arrangements, and power of attorney for medical and physical assets. I found that this "process" ends at the grave, not at the final breath.

Chapter Ten: "Death is a Process"

Heavenly Father, this situation and process still brings tears to my eyes and feelings of brokenness in my heart. This process was so hard to go through. I pray for the one who is in the same experience and needing Your touch, Your help and guidance to make it through another day, another appointment, another step in the "process."

Chapter Eleven: Pick Your Battles

> Psalm 62:5 NLT, "Let all that I am wait quietly before God for my help is in him."

During this LTC process you learn to pick your battles! You learn to fly your surrender flag to certain things that change in relevance or even argument. Sometimes well-intentioned family and friends would say things that clearly showed that they weren't involved in my mom's or brother's care. I gave up pressing my mom to choose better foods to eat and not so many snacks. I controlled that with the type of snacks that I bought for her. Eliminating chocolate was not going to be an optional "surrender," so I purchased smaller size chocolates, i.e., kisses. Some battles were not in my control.

I wished I could raise the surrender flag to COVID regulations. My mother would rather have gotten COVID than to not be able to see, hug, kiss and visit her family. It was at the time of COVID that she literally lost the sparkle in her eyes, and I remember the day she did just that. The grandchildren and I visited her in a very noisy outside environment. She had a hard time hearing us. We were six feet apart with plexiglass in between us and literally roped off on the side to ensure that no one crossed the lines of permission. She could not hear us. It was a thirty-minute visit. I will never forget the moment that she was wheeled away that day. Her brown eyes were sad and for the first time I didn't see that spark in her eyes. They were lifeless and she rolled away a different person.

Maybe it isn't COVID that you've had to experience in long-term care. I experienced other battles in each facility. All were understaffed and overworked. There was not always enough time for the little things that needed to be addressed. Bathroom visits were difficult to manage with the lack of staff. I saw many tears of embarrassment on behalf of the residents.

Lord, my prayer today comes from a heart that feels broken from the continual decision of this battle zone of long-term care. Our family members cannot perform the simple life tasks any longer for themselves and must depend on others and on their timing. Give us wisdom in the battles that we face. Help us to feel that You are in our midst and that You know our needs.

Chapter Twelve: Brokenness and Suffering

> Ephesians 6:13 NIV, "Put on the whole armor of God that when the day of evil comes, you may be able to stand your ground, and after you have done everything, to stand."

THERE WERE SO MANY EXPERIENCES OF THE DEEP feelings in my heart of brokenness and suffering. I had constant feelings of a stabbing pain straight into the heart. Here are a few examples:

- Removing my mom from her home of 65 years.
- Two years COVID lockdowns with long-term effects.
- Falls, injuries, broken bones, surgeries.
- Watching dementia take a life that was joyful.
- Constant medical decisions.
- Signing admittance applications for long-term care.
- Selling and or removing possessions of a lifetime.
- Hearing the question "Where is my dog?"

- Cognitive decline. Conversations used to be lively.
- Sadness running through your heart as they wheel away silent.
- Witnessing them dying.
- Funerals. Saying goodbye. Forever.

Dear Heavenly Faither, my heart is with those reading this devotion. My heart hurts repeatedly as I relive this experience, but I am grateful to be able to use this platform and the last five years to help someone else to maneuver through this battlefield of pain, suffering, brokenness, and sorrow. Help us to remember that You are with us and equip us for the challenges.

Chapter Thirteen: GUILT

Proverbs 17:22 KJV, "A merry heart doeth good like a medicine: but a broken spirit drieth the bones."

GUILT. IS IT A NOUN OR A VERB? IS IT A FACT OR A feeling? I've been in this season now for two and a half years. I remember the guilt that I felt when I had to make the decision for my mom to live in long-term care. It was the first day there. I had gotten her settled in her room and surroundings. She was required to use a wheelchair all the time for her safety. Her room was very clean, with large windows at her level of sight. I left her to get acquainted with her roommate and to take a break from all that I was feeling in that room.

I came back later in the evening to comfort her one more time, or in all honesty, to comfort myself! I could see her wheelchair up to her bed and out lay her Bible on it to read. Guilt flooded my soul! Tears filled my eyes. My heart felt broken in many pieces to see that she was looking to Jesus and the comfort of His word in a situation that she couldn't control.

There were many more times of feeling overwhelmed with guilt when I would hear comments from the family that she didn't belong there. Additional times of hearing my mom question me of how her beloved dog was doing and where was he? The holidays always positioned me to feel the overwhelming, repeated, and gut-wrenching feeling of guilt once again.

Prayer: Oh, Heavenly Father, this day I lift my heart to You. It feels broken in many pieces, With a stabbing pain like it is punctured. I ask that You deliver me from the feelings of guilt that plague me in this situation. My spirit feels broken; I ask that You lift me out of this pit and lead me to the feelings of a merry heart. Thank You for holding me together through these situations. Thank You that my mom's reaction today was to look to You and meditate on Your Word. I am grateful for Your promises.

Chapter Fourteen: Resources That Help

Hebrews 13:5 NIV, "… I will never leave you nor forsake you."

I WAS VISITING WITH FRIENDS IN ONE OF THE Amish living communities in Ohio. Each visit includes a favorite Christian bookstore there. We usually get lost in there for hours as we look through all the books, Bible markers, journals, gifts, etc. and seeking the perfect book or magazine to support our present walk with the Lord. I purchased a book that had pictures of coffee cups lined up with decreasing color in each cup until the last one was empty. It was a book written by a son of a mother who had dementia and was written the last four years of their lives together. It was sort of a diary or journal written by the son about his decisions and visits together. He identified the personal struggles of guilt and brokenness including the time that he had to move her out of state and to a local long-term care facility closest to where he lived.

I am writing this small devotional experiencing that there aren't many resources out there to not only help you (i.e., when you must consult an elder attorney) but also to add some sanity to your broken heart, quick decisions, and a turnaround in everyone's life that is affected.

Prayer: With great thankfulness and gratefulness, Lord, I acknowledge You provide what we need, and Your timing amazes me. As we look to You, I ask that You place the timely resources needed in the lives of those who are needing help. For those that are feeling alone through this journey, I pray that they would continually feel your presence and peace.

Chapter Fifteen: New Titles, Decisions and End of Life

> Philippians 4:7 NIV, "And the peace of God, which transcends all human understanding, will guard your hearts and your minds in Christ Jesus."

It had been two and one-half years into this experience and feeling of brokenness. My heart is always filled with grief for both my mom and brother.

The first thing I had to do was to obtain a power of attorney (POA) to handle all their financial and medical affairs, house utilities, doctor appointments, and each of them were on limited income.

Living wills had to be written and attorney appointments made to guide me. It felt like I was intruding in their personal lives. I was the younger sibling who was never able to "tell my brother what to do," if you can catch my drift here.

I have repeatedly and out loud said to God, "I don't want this title!" Life responsibilities for two people at the same time and both in long-term care was overwhelming me.

My experience of the last five years... In the beginning one thing that I did not realize about possessing the "titles", i.e., power of attorney, caregiver and executor was what they fully meant until I became the executor, specifically for my brother. You see, at the end of his life, he was in the ER with seventy percent of his body septic. The doctors giving him antibiotics and pain meds hoping that he could recover in time placed me in a position to basically make a life-or-death decision for him. It was March 2022. I had to make the decision as POA of in- hospital hospice care or continuing the regime of hospitalized meds and maybe returning to the nursing facility.

This was a tearful time of seeking the Lord for direction. Knowing that my brother had asked Jesus into his life and indicated that he was ready to meet his wife, our mom and dad in heaven didn't make any of this easier. I finally had peace and authority through the title of medical power of attorney; I made the decision for end-of-life hospice care. I knew that was what he would want. Not to return to the nursing facility, but to enter the gates of heaven from the hospital.

Prayer: Lord, my heart is racing. I am exhausted. I surrender this fight. I ask for Your peace that passes all human understanding. I place my brother in Your hands and if my decision is the wrong one, then I know that You will raise him up from this bed and deliver him from this septic state.

Chapter Sixteen: Stress – Taking Care of Yourself

2 Timothy 1:7 NIV, "For the Spirit God gave us does not make us timid, but gives us power, love, and self-discipline."

I HAVE A BLACK AND WHITE PICTURE OF A HOMEless man on my desk. The words printed on it are "Nothing Changes Until Something Changes." I always need a new mindset when considering exercise to eliminate or to relieve stress. Intentions are high. I may even purchase new workout wear just to get me in the mood. When an individual is under this much stress, it begins to take its toll. I find that fast food becomes the normal to save time. Walking outdoors and breathing in oxygen and absorbing the sunshine can eliminate the feelings of stress. Meditating or a yoga class teaches you how to breathe properly and to set your mind to something else, a very much needed practice in this season of life. I would also suggest a vacation of some sort away from everyone. Time is needed to just converse with God. Cast your cares upon Him. Surrender all that you are carrying. Psalm

23 is a continual mindset renewal for me and I think that you will find it to be the same.

Looking back, I needed to do what I needed first; you know, put your oxygen mask on first, then help the person next to you!

Dear Lord Jesus, I have battled much with declines in my health and inclines with stress levels, anxiety, and brokenness. Help me today to live for today, to focus on healthy habits for my life, healthy foods and exercise that energize and motivate me. Thank You for another day.

Chapter Seventeen: A "New Normal"

Psalm 138:8 KJV, "The Lord will perfect that which concerns me."

A TERM THAT DESCRIBES THIS SEASON AND HAS become repetitive is a "new normal," describing the tasks and living that was normal, to now a new normal. I look at it in two lifestyles, one for the resident and one for the family, friend, or caretaker.

Starting with the resident: a new normal is that nothing in life is the same after entering long-term care. You moved into a new place, most of the time against your will. You share a room with a stranger. There is no more grocery shopping. Food is prepared for you that wasn't your recipe or even your selection. There is a shared bathroom with your roommate and other rooms. Your schedule to bathe and dress is set for you. You are told where you eat and when you eat. A vending machine is sometimes provided for snacks. There are loud television noises from other rooms; this is especially challenging to deal with if the other residents are hard of hearing. There are unwelcome odors. Hair and doctor appointments and even transportation is now a New Normal. Sadly, I must add lack of church services and communion is a new Normal.

Family, friend, or caretaker: you now juggle schedules of work and other family and now add visits in your schedule. Extra time is now added to your visit if you stop at a convenience store for favorite snacks or room decorations. Your social media updates request prayers, cards, sharing health updates or pictures. You find that you schedule additional doctor appointments for yourself as you become affected with headaches, stomach issues, and insomnia. Added to this list are the appointments and completion of paperwork for power of attorney and other new responsibilities. The list is unending.

Lord, I am grateful that I can pray about everything and worry about nothing. I stand on Your promises of Psalm 138:8 to perfect that which concerns me. I've prayed this prayer for finances, car problems, and now at this time of change in the stage/season that life is no longer normal.

Chapter Eighteen: Heaven's Roll Call

2 Timothy 4:7 NIV, "I have fought the good fight. I have finished the race. I have kept the faith."

It was Thursday, September 10, 2020, that I was called to the hospital by the ER doctor in the wee hours of the morning. My mom was much distressed with sepsis coma, organ failure, a hematoma, and much more with the outlook of a slow process to get her back to baselines. She had no focus or recognition that I was present. Her breathing was aggressive, and I had never been in this situation before. I met with the doctor who directed me to arrange for hospice care.

My mom was a Christian woman who longed to leave this earth and be with Jesus. She once told me that when she died, don't pray her back because she is going to Heaven and see Jesus and all her loved ones. Then she would reassure me that she loved me, and she knew that I understood that she didn't want to suffer.

I turned the background music of hymns on my mobile phone and placed it where she could hear them. I kept trying to get her to focus on me, but she did not. I sat next to her, praying, for the next hour. Her breathing began to be more peaceful and was not racing any longer. Eventually, she slept and at her last breath, I perceive that she walked right into heaven. I wonder if there is a roll call in heaven because I know that on Thursday, September 10th, 2020, Geraldine L. Moore was called into heaven.

There is no doubt in my mind that my mom went straight to meet Jesus and then on to join the angel choir.

Prayer: Lord Jesus, what a privilege and broken heart at the same time to be present for my mom's last breath. Thank You that the hymns are still available to usher our loved ones into heaven. Thank You that my mom is no longer suffering and is now free, healthy, and happy and my assumption is that she went straight to heaven's choir!

Chapter Nineteen: It's the Small Things

1 Peter 3:12 NIV, "The eyes of the Lord watch over those who do right, and his ears are open to their prayers."

My mom had been gone for about 15 days at this time. As I went through her treasures from the long-term care facility, I realized the things that meant the most to her were small things. I always kept her stocked with small chocolates and her favorite soda in her container of three drawers in the closet. Her picture collage was always a point of conversation with everyone, and she was proud of it. Her favorite color was pink and so was her Bible written in the King James Version. I found the stack of cards that I would read to her over and over. The artwork from her daily activities hung on the clothespin line that we made for her to display her creations. The costume jewelry and holiday-themed clothing in the closet was a reminder of how much she liked to be dressed up. Each holiday brought a new door wreath and room decorations. A new bed comforter would brighten and change things up as well.

Prayer: Heavenly Father, how grateful we are that You meet our every need. Sometimes the heart aches a little more, like on the holidays. Thank You for the inspiration of the small things that we can do for our loved ones. Bless their rooms with joy and Your presence. Send Your angels to minister to them when we can't be there. Hear their prayers and answer them. Thank You for your abundant love for them.

Chapter Twenty: Jesus Loves the Little Children and So Do the Elderly

I Corinthians 13:7 NLT, "Love never gives up, never loses faith, is always hopeful, and endures every circumstance."

WE TRIED TO PROTECT THE CHILDREN FROM FEELings of disappointment, hurt and feeling sad to see Mom a.k.a. Mumal, in this setting versus the visits to their homes where they would play outside in her yard or swing on the outdoor swing. My mother couldn't wait to see the children. She loved that the youngest would crawl up in her bed to play with her decorative pillows. They would trade pushing her around in her wheelchair. My mom particularly enjoyed seeing the youngest one in her dance outfit or tutu going to practice after the visit. The local dance groups would come and perform in the dining room. The Boy Scouts would come in uniform and badges and earn their Community Service patch by serving at the Christmas dinner. Many churches were involved, with Sunday Schools making cards or small book markers and placing them at each seat in the dining room for the residents to take back to their rooms. My grandchildren loved to color and especially paint with my mom. She absorbed every minute of their visits with joy.

Prayer: Lord, help us to remain conscious of the things that would make our loved ones smile. Provide the opportunities to bring them joy in their lives. Give us words to share with them that encourage them and tell them that they are loved.

Chapter Twenty-One: Memories

Matthew 5:16 KJV, "Let your light so shine before men, that they may see your good works, and glorify your Father who is in Heaven."

THERE IS A CHALLENGE TO BEING AND DOING creative things that will make your loved one feel at home or remind them of their lives, but not to the extent it keeps them yearning to go back home. It takes putting on a creative hat to figure out what memories you would like to keep current and those that may be too heartbreaking of a reminder of their life before long-term care.

My brother was a volunteer fireman at our local fire department. He always wore his ballcap from the fire department. As are most other volunteers for a non-profit organization, he was very proud of the fire station, trucks and all that comes with it. I downloaded a picture of that fire department truck from their website and framed it for him to sit on his dresser.

Creating a memory may backfire a time or two! My mother loved her wall picture collage in her room. It made conversation with everyone, and she was so proud of her family. However, my brother said, "No, I'm not staying here. I'm going home" to my suggestion that I make him one.

The great-grandchildren had fun with sand art pictures and framed them for her windowsill. They were made with beautiful colors and white frames and matting. There was always something to look at that was joyful or reminded her that we loved her and would be back to visit her.

For years my sister-in-law would decorate the residents' doors at the facility for Christmas with her own materials and supplies.

A friend of mine is a seamstress and quilter. We converted one of my father's company logo shirts into a memory bear that now sits in my office. The pattern pieces are free online. I am sure that there are many other memory opportunities that I am not even aware of.

Small things matter. I am wondering, what ideas can you share with me that you found successful?

Prayer: Dear Heavenly Father, I am grateful for all Your provisions during this season of brokenness, provisions of support with activity departments, volunteers, and free ideas offered online. Make us aware of what our loved one needs to help them reject their thoughts of disappointment and brokenness. Provide those things and people to shine Your light.

Chapter Twenty-Two: A New Set of Wheels

Esther 4:14 NIV,
"And who knows but that you have come to your royal position for such a time as this?"

THE FEELING OF SEEING MY BROTHER IN A WHEELchair at the age of 62, being unable to walk, broke my heart over and over at each visit and each conversation. The entire right side of his body was paralyzed. Rehabilitation was scheduled and filled us with hope in each session even though the outcomes that we wanted weren't possible. I attended every care meeting for him. I constantly asked, "What can I do for him to make life easier?" Each time I was in tears. My stomach was a mess and my mind would not shut off until I found something to help him.

I spent many hours praying for my brother and asking God for creative ideas that would help or improve his life and health. What would make his challenges easier to manage? I met with the physical therapy professionals and asked if we could customize a wheelchair for him that fit his needs of having to sit in it all day and into the evening. He needed one that reclined if he wanted to rest from a sitting position, with a leg lift to add comfort to the right leg and that would strap his foot into place since atrophy had set in. It needed a tray to hold the right arm in place. Most importantly, a cushioned seat!! And as God often will answer specific prayers, it was his favorite color, blue! The wheels turned easier, and he was able to manage it by himself.

Maybe a wheelchair isn't your answer to making life easier for your loved one. Do an assessment of thoughts that create a conversation in the care meeting that will help you to satisfy your concerns and improve their health.

I am presently remembering the suggestion and purchase of an iPad. There are free puzzles, art, and other programs that usually offer different levels starting with beginner. We would enjoy puzzles on it, and he didn't realize that I was trying to keep his cognitive skills at their peak.

Prayer: Lord, Jesus, there are times when seeing the results of a stroke or diseases like dementia in the young and old can cause feelings of brokenness and discouragement. Many times, we don't know how to fill the desire of knowing how to help them. Give us wisdom and clarity of their needs so that we can assist and know that we can speak up for the helpless. Help me to be grateful that You chose me and specifically for "such a time as this."

Chapter Twenty-Three: 'Tis the Season – Room and Holiday Decorations

Matthew 7:12 NKJV, "Therefore, whatever you want men to do to you, do also to them."

Holidays were the most difficult for me. Nothing is quite normal. Your loved one is in a different environment, not surrounded by traditional meals and family gatherings. I did try to visit the morning of the holiday and make sure that my mom had her "themed" attire, hair accessories and jewelry to celebrate. Next, I would decorate her door, room, and bed to match the occasion. I added a CD player for her to hear holiday music in the background. She wasn't much of a TV watcher, nor could she maneuver the remote control (tears!)

The struggle was still real. The activities directors played an important role at holidays, always providing entertainment, fun, games, and decorations with the hope of bringing a festive feeling on those days. I still felt broken.

I had a conversation with the activities director about a few of their activities and discovered that they have a very limited budget to work with and they really do their best. She shared with me that they can accept gift cards to local department stores that sell the supplies. You can also purchase supplies like art projects, give aways, and nail polish for spa days. They create a monthly calendar for you to follow with the activities. I encourage you to get a copy of it. Take a picture of it with your phone and it makes it a great resource to be on the same page with what is being offered. Oh, before I forget this one! Themed cupcakes are always a hit— and share with the staff to celebrate!

Prayer: Dear Heavenly Father, the Golden Rule is the do unto others as you would want them to do unto you. I pray that we remain sensitive to celebrate and to care even more on the holidays in long-term care facilities. Give us ideas to keep the holidays special, festive looking and inclusive.

Chapter Twenty-Four: Gift of Giving: Birthdays, Special Occasions, Etc.

Ephesians 5:16 NIV, "Make the most of every opportunity."

You never lose the joy over cupcakes and balloons! Oh, you can add flowers too!! Remember that not all residents can eat sugar so have something for them too. The staff is great at improvising so that all can participate.

All our lives, families celebrate birthdays and special occasions. The last time I checked, Valentine's Day was expected to bring in $25.9 billion dollars to celebrate our LOVE for one another. Those heart shaped boxes of candies bring an instant smile to your loved one and share your message of how much you love them without words.

Baskets of various themes have taken over gift giving from wrapped boxes and bows. Baskets can also be given at any celebration. My mom was in her eighties, and we still made her an Easter basket filled with her favorite things. She also requested me to bring one for her roommate and for another lady who was her friend. Coloring books, crayons, pencils, bookmarks, small art projects to complete all wrapped up in a basket were such a blessing to them and truly changed the atmosphere to one of celebration.

Many church ladies' groups would stuff lunch size bags in various colors with these items and give them to the residents who had attended their church for various occasions.

It is heartbreaking at times to celebrate wedding anniversaries or other milestones. You try to stay away from bringing up things that would remind them of home and other personal memories, but I find that they enjoy talking about the past, their growing up, recipes, and even your days as a child.

Holidays like Thanksgiving offer an opportunity to visit them with their favorite flavor of pie. My mom's selection was lemon, and it was guaranteed to be a win-win at those visits.

Prayer: Gracious Lord and Savior, thank You for providing times of celebration with our loved ones. Help me to be a blessing to them and give me ideas that are personal to bring joy and celebration in this season of time and life. Help me to be aware of making the most of every opportunity that arises.

Chapter Twenty-Five: Isolation and Deterioration (Covid 19)

Psalm 46:1 KJV, "God is our refuge and strength, a very present help in trouble."

IN THE YEAR OF 2020, COVID 19 WAS RELEASED, causing a world pandemic. A health war began as COVID 19 patients were moved into long-term care nursing homes to live, and hospitals were overcrowded. Some hospitals used outside tents to care for sick patients. At the beginning of the pandemic, the virus spread throughout these facilities, which resulted in over 6000 deaths in the state of PA where I live.

Harsh regulations were then set, and, in my opinion, my mom and many other residents died of COVID 19 from the inside out! They were isolated and under quarantine immediately. Masks were mandatory. Fear began to set in their hearts. Social activities came to an abrupt halt. All meals were served in their rooms. No dining room socialization. No cosmetologist or barber appointments for their grooming. Most importantly to my mom was that there were no clergy visits, communion, scheduled musicians, or prayer groups were permitted. My mom's life, stripped of family and faith, was now replaced by fear. It was at that time, March 2020, that my mom began to decline.

I remember the last visit with her during COVID regulations that I claim was the day that I witnessed her to physically and mentally check out of this wonderful life that we had enjoyed. It was an outside visit, six feet apart. A roped off barrier and plexiglass in between us. Everyone masked. She couldn't hear our conversation with outside background noises. She didn't understand that we couldn't hug her. I brought her the usual goody bag that she always appreciated and she would pull each item out and comment. Except that day. Her attendant wheeled her away, with no words, the unopened bag sitting on her lap. No smile or hug. It still brings tears to my eyes while typing this story and remembering the details of literally the day that my mom checked out of life.

Prayer: Lord, I am forever grateful that Your promises cover broken hearts. I feel like I can't do this day. My heart is so broken for my mom and others in these long-term care facilities that don't understand or comprehend this time of life. I pray that they will feel Your presence in their rooms. I pray that their hearts will be warmed with Your love and that You would continue to minister to them through the staff, television, and radio programs during this time that we are cut out of their lives.

Chapter Twenty-Six: Transition – It's a Process

Psalm 23:1 NKJV, "The Lord is my Shepherd, I shall not want."

I'VE CRIED SO MANY TIMES THROUGHOUT THIS season of brokenness. I felt that every new thing was overwhelming and shattered my heart. I never thought of the word "transition" before, the process of or a period of changing from one state or condition to another. It came quite quickly, without a warning, and stayed for a long time.

My brother and his transition needs were not the same as my mom's. My mom was leaving her home after a lifetime at the same address. She was not leaving as a volunteer, and it was going to be a permanent transition. My mother had a great relationship with her church pastor, and I recruited him to visit my mom with me at the hospital to help me to share the news with her that she wasn't going home. She would be changing residences and her dog was not part of the transition. Needless to say, and again, I was totally broken and could not announce this news to her. Especially since she was already worried about my brother and how he was doing.

Questions were running through her mind, i.e., is he still alive? Where is he? Thankfully, her focus wasn't on herself as much as being worried about him.

To transition to a long-term care facility, the biggest challenge is selecting which facility for your loved one. It is a big challenge to make the move as seamless as possible. Was it even possible to create a loving and warm home environment without all that is left at home? I realize now that I needed a support team who had been through this before to help me navigate this transition process when I was suffering personally from so much brokenness. Next, the biggest transition is moving in. Is she going to like having a roommate now that shares pretty much everything? Questions run through your mind of how you can make this room and facility feel more like home.

I mentioned my brother earlier, that his outlook on transitioning was not the same as our mom's. He was transported from the hospital to a rehab facility and from day one of being admitted he never accepted transitioning to life there or any other facility. In his mind, he was going home, and five years later that hope inside of him never left.

Prayer: Father, I look to the 23rd Psalm that reminds me that You provide all that I need, that You protect me and watch over me. At this very difficult time and with a feeling of utter brokenness, I ask that the Holy Spirit remind my mom and brother that You will never leave them. I am thankful for Your promises of comfort, strength, anointing and presence... all the days of my life.

Chapter Twenty-Seven: How to Make a No Sew Tied Blanket

Psalm 118:24 NLT, "This is the day that the Lord has made. We will rejoice and be glad in it."

I THOUGHT I WOULD SHARE ONE OF OUR IDEAS that we used to decorate my mom's room and to make it as personal as possible. We made tied blankets using different patterns, colors, and fabrics. It takes very little time, and the size determines how much material it takes. (We also made these blankets in our church ladies' groups and then donated them to non-profit organizations to distribute).

ITEMS NEEDED:

- 2 pieces of fleece 1 – 1/14 yards each
- Fabric scissors (or a rotary cutter – easier!)
- Flat cutting surface (I use my dining room table)
- Ruler

1. Step One. Lay the two fabric pieces wrong sides together.
2. Step Two. With the fabric pieces on top of each other, trim off any ends as necessary to make them the same size.
3. Step Three. Use a rotary cutter or scissors (I use) and cut right along the edge of your ruler to make sure that both pieces are the same size. (There is usually extra on one of the pieces from the bolt end, etc.)
4. Step Four. Cut out a square size of 3 inches on each corner (to make it lay flat and not bunch up).
5. Step Five. Using fabric scissors, cut strips through both fabrics and all the way down the sides, each about ½ inch wide and 3 inches deep. (If the strips are too short, they will not tie together well).
6. Step Six. Tie the top and bottom strips together in a double knot (keeps it from coming apart in the wash).
7. Step Seven. Continue all the way around until your blanket is complete!
8. Step Eight. Using a permanent marker, write their name on the blanket (eliminates hours of looking for it after the wash!)

There are several tutorials online if this is your first introduction to making a fleece tied blanket.

CHAPTER TWENTY-SEVEN: HOW TO MAKE A NO SEW TIED BLANKET

Prayer: I pray, Lord Jesus, that my loved one will feel loved and blessed with this homemade gift. I pray that every time that they lay it on themselves or fold it on the foot of their bed that You would flood wonderful memories through their minds and hearts. I thank You for a good day today and that we will share many more good days. I pray that we will rejoice and be glad in this day and every day.

Chapter Twenty-Eight: What Do Faith, Church, Ministries, and Pets Have in Common?

1 Corinthians 13:4-5 NIV, "Love is patient. Love is kind. It does not envy. It does not boast, it is not proud. It does not dishonor others. It is not self-seeking. It is not easily angered. It keeps no record of wrongs."

WHAT DO FAITH, CHURCH, MINISTRIES, AND PETS have in common? LOVE! Yes, one simple word. One simple act of service. A place to visit and love that surrounds you. Attendance in a congregation of people who love you, including our furry, or not so furry pets, who love you too.

My family grew up attending church services, choir practices, and other events. I've seen quite a few singing quartets in my younger days of attending with my mother or even watching them on the television. Each summer was youth camp and once a week was choir practice. Other ministries in the area would offer concerts and annual tent revivals. Each of these played a role in living a Christian lifestyle in our home.

I have a picture of myself at the age of two or three taken in the church nursery. I would sit in the pews with my mom and grandmother when my feet barely fit to the end of the seat. Each pew was made of wood with book holders for the hymnals. Growing up through the years, our church became the epitome of love to us and even to the death of my mom and brother. My mom was old fashioned and traditional; her deceased body lay in the casket at the altar of her church. This was a place, once again, where you felt the love of each one who attended the viewing or sent flowers and gifts.

I must expound a little on the love of our pets because she loved her dog, Duce, and he loved her! They shared their love in so many personal ways. Duce would lay on her lap. I know he was protecting her, but he also provided warmth to her while sleeping on her lap. She would spoil him by giving him snacks that he probably should not have had. And I must mention how much love you feel from your pets when you leave and return. Their welcome greeting of their love to see you is not always describable in words.

Prayer: Thank You, Lord, that You are the example of love to us, to give Your life for us at the cross. Love can be described in so many ways and felt through so many things. Help me to share Your love with those who are broken. I pray that I will continue to look for ways to show Your love to others and if they do not know you, that the Holy Spirit will draw them to Your unconditional and everlasting love.

Chapter Twenty-Nine: It's a Beautiful Day. Rediscover Life

Psalm 16:11 NIV, "You make known to me the path of life; you will fill me with joy in your presence, with eternal pleasures at your right hand."

My mom reached the place in life where she was able to accept long-term living and care. Her church and pastors remained faithful to visit and bring communion each week. She loved the socializing and activities. It took a little creativity to facilitate living in the same room with a stranger. We had to rediscover life. Sit outside. Go for a wheelchair ride. Put a bird feeder outside the window of her room. Open the blinds! It's a beautiful day! I had to believe that first, so that my mom would allow it to happen in her life.

As I reflect on that season, I learned a few things about life. I have often heard others say, "Enjoy life while you can." Even in the books of Proverbs and Psalms many scriptures speak of living life. Allow me to encourage you who are reading these devotionals: there is light at the end of this season of brokenness, guilt, sadness, and anxiety. You must first care for yourself. Remember, you must put your oxygen mask on first before helping anyone else. I didn't do that and wow, did I pay the price with my health. My anxiety was at the highest level I have ever experienced. The way to survive it all is having a personal relationship with Jesus Christ and not only reading His Word but believing that it is true. Pray these scriptures that I have shared with each step of this path and season. Pray the prayers for yourself and your season.

Prayer: Good morning, Lord Jesus. When I was young, we sang the lyrics of a song that said "It's a happy day and I thank God for the weather. It's a happy day and I'm living it for my Lord." Today, I pray that I will feel that happiness. It has been a while. Thank You for the feeling of some peace today and for the path of rediscovering life. Thank You for a smile from my mom today and hearing her say "I love you."

Chapter Thirty: Life is Like a Box of Chocolates

Jeremiah 29:11 NIV, "I know the plans that I have for you, declares the Lord, plans to prosper you and not to harm you, plans to give you hope and a future."

Your life has already been determined, if you believe Jeremiah 29:11. God knew you before you were born. He has a plan for you, a plan of hope and success.

When I open a box of chocolates, the first temptation is the welcoming packaging, then the aroma reaches your nostrils and the printed guide temps you to grab your favorite. Sometimes, you bite your least favorite or smash the bottom of the chocolate to have a peek at what is inside.

Life is the same way to me. I've learned that life is in chapters. Each chapter is different. There are great ones and there are not so great ones, and we are not in control.

Each of us is given one life to live. Make good choices, including your health choices. My brother's stroke was the result of high blood pressure that was unattended and hence a brain bleed and stroke that changed all our lives.

I would like to give a small box of chocolates with this book or even to include a scratch and sniff card to experience and save in your memory bank this moment of time. Your piece of chocolate today may be in celebration of something. It may be a little peace from a tough situation. It could be a reminder of a memory, the small things or even a reward to yourself of the new normal.

Prayer: Dear Heavenly Father, I come to You this day with a thankful heart, thankful that You have never left me through all of this. Thankful that You carried me when I felt that I couldn't do it anymore. Thankful that You provided everything that I needed and in many ways. I am grateful to now have learned that You have a plan for me and these last five years You have carried me. I am not the same person I once was. I've been changed, strengthened, and blessed.

Chapter Thirty-One: Final Chapter – William's Death

John 3:16 KJV, "For God so loved the world that he gave his only begotten son, that whosoever believeth in him should not perish but have everlasting life."

IT WAS MARCH 19, 2022. THE EMERGENCY ROOM doctor's call was not foreign to me in reference to my brother. Again, his symptoms were seventy percent sepsis, UTI and kidney infections, a diagnosis all too common for him. Only this time was worse. I often complained to God about the title of power of attorney. I didn't want the responsibility that came with it. My brother had never let me control his decisions and I didn't want the control now. The choices given were to stay with the antibiotics to try to heal his body and return to long-term care. He still was paralyzed on his right side. He did not have the independence that he wanted. I could see the brokenness in his eyes when we talked about his visitation schedule and there were no others scheduled but mine. He was tired and very sick. The doctor conversations ended with hospice care in the hospital. I struggled with the medical decisions this time and the weight of the title of power of attorney was greater this time than anything else that I had to do for my brother's care. With POA, I had to make the decision of end-of-life care, hospital hospice or weeks of the meds to heal the body. I made the most difficult, heart wrenching decision: end-of-life care, based on our conversations with him that he did not want to suffer anymore. He assured me and others that he was ready to die. My prayer and conversation with the Lord were to the point. "Lord, if I am wrong here, either my brother will rise out of this bed, or You will take him home and free him from all this brokenness and suffering." Three days later, March 22, 2022, at ten fifty-five p.m., Jesus called him home.

Prayer: Lord, it has been a long, hard season filled with brokenness and even death. I have been taught in scripture to run this race and look towards the prize of heaven and eternity. I have learned so much on this journey, and that You are with us. You promised to never leave us. Earthly circumstances may look like the opposite of that belief. I have learned to have courage. I have learned to trust You and I can only pray that I fulfilled my purpose. This chapter of life is finished.

END

Printed in the USA
CPSIA information can be obtained
at www.ICGtesting.com
LVHW020443300824
789570LV00003B/11